All Scripture references taken from the KJV of the Holy Bible, unless otherwise indicated.

the spirit of error: paving the way for antichrist

Dr. Marlene Miles

Freshwater Press 2025

freshwaterpress9@gmail.com

ISBN: ISBN: 978-1-965772-98-0

Paperback Version

Copyright 2025, Dr. Marlene Miles

All rights reserved. No part of this book may be reproduced, distributed, or transmitted by any means or in any means including photocopying, recording or other electronic or mechanical methods without prior written permission of the publisher except in the case of brief publications or critical reviews.

Table of Contents

Error 4

Secret Faults 9

Lying Voices 13

Flattery 18

Fake Holy Spirit 24

Test the Spirits 33

The Very Elect 37

The Final Antichrist 42

False Tongues 46

Don't Chase Gifts 56

Attributes of the Holy Spirit 68

Fruit of the Spirit 72

Voices 76

Real Love 84

Prayers 97

Dear Reader 114

Prayerbooks by this author 115

Other books by this author 117

the spirit of error

Error

Beloved, believe not every spirit, but try the spirits whether they are of God: because many false prophets are gone out into the world.
Hereby know ye the Spirit of God: Every spirit that confesseth that Jesus Christ is come in the flesh is of God:
And every spirit that confesseth not that Jesus Christ is come in the flesh is not of God: and this is that spirit of antichrist, whereof ye have heard that it should come; and even now already is it in the world.
Ye are of God, little children, and have overcome them: because greater is he that is in you, than he that is in the world.
They are of the world: therefore speak they of the world, and the world heareth them. (1 John 4:1-5)

This book is about the *spirit of error*. Error is a falling away or deviation from the truth; a mistake in judgment, such as believing what is not true. *Error* may be voluntary, or involuntary. A person could be tricked into error, or make an honest mistake.

We need to: Say not, it was an *error*. (Ecclesiastes 5:6). We must be steadfast and know the Word and not let ourselves be blown about by winds of doctrine, the great swelling words of liars, false prophets, false pastors, even antichrists, and the final antichrist. The Antichrist, the man of lawlessness is coming to deceive mankind and set up his own kingdom. This is akin to the devil thinking he won again. However, the Antichrist will be allowed for a season; that season will be called the Great Tribulation. But just as the devil thought he had defeated Jesus on the Cross, he was and will ultimately be sorely disappointed. The spirit of error is essential in paving the way for the final Antichrist.

God wins. We win. But until that time the Man of Lawlessness comes to deceive the whole world which has been the devil's game plan all along.

The Antichrist will set up a new religion, establishing himself as a deity and the head of that religion. Those who refuse to obey the Antichrist will face severe penalties, including economic sanctions and death.

Uh, folks, I kinda suspect that the Antichrist won't call himself the Antichrist. Most likely he will call himself something that is the very opposite of anti-Christ. We will have to either see it with our eyes, hear it with our ears, or discern it with our *Discerner*. That's why trying the *spirits* right now is really good practice, just in case we are still here when all this goes down. No one knows the day or the hour of his ascension to power, but even the Bible warned over and again what the last days would look like, and it looks like we might be in those days, at least to this author.

Nebuchadnezzar created an image, and it was mandatory for Daniel and his three Hebrew friends to bow and worship it. They did not and were thrown in the Fiery Furnace; but God saved them. When King Darius decreed that no one was to pray to anyone, any *god,* or anything other than the king for 30 days and Daniel didn't obey, Daniel was thrown into the Lion's Den; but God saved him.

Will you be so upright before the Lord as Daniel was that if anything like that were to happen to you, you would trust that God would save you, or die believing God? Would you refuse to bow because of your dedication to the Lord?

The false prophet, who works alongside the Antichrist, will create an image of the Beast and compel people to worship it.

Because of the signs it was given power to perform on behalf of the first beast, it

deceived the inhabitants of the earth. It ordered them to set up an image in honor of the beast who was wounded by the sword and yet lived.
The second beast was given power to give breath to the image of the first beast, so that the image could speak and cause all who refused to worship the image to be killed. (Revelation 13)

Walking by sight not only gets people into mega trouble, but it also displeases God. It is easy to deceive sight walkers, all you have to do is create the image that they want to see or the image that they will believe. Just make the image or the images look like them, look like something that they will accept, or make it look like something they want to be, something they aspire to be or make it something shiny, pretty, and expensive. A golden calf? Humans love idols. Voila! In Scripture and theology, *error* is sin; iniquity; transgression. The Antichrist is coming with *error* and to lead the whole world into *error*. Until that time, many antichrists have arisen; it says so even in the Bible.

Secret Faults

Who can understand his errors? Cleanse thou me from secret faults. (Psalms 19:12)

What is a secret fault? It is sins that you don't even know you committed because you don't know the Word of God, all of us have probably been guilty of that. Or, a secret fault or secret error could occur because you believe a lie and go down the wrong path, that is a result of error.

Error could be hidden sins that you are collected from being in association and relationship with sinners, unknowingly. There is such a thing as the transfer of *spirits*. Hidden sins, hidden faults, hidden *errors* are possible.

Man can fall into error when he is listening to the wrong *voices*. There are so many voices that want our attention, and we must be wise to try these *spirits* to see if they are of God. Ask yourself,

- Does God talk like this?
- Would God say anything like this?
- Has God in times past EVER said anything like this?

Secret sins are a bit different than hidden sins. Secret sins are transgressions a person commits and seeks to cover up or hide. Hidden sins are sins that are even hidden to the perpetrator of that sin; they don't even realize they sinned, until some later day or date, or ever in some cases. (More on this in my book, **Hidden Sins: Hidden Iniquity**. https://a.co/d/4WW4jOy)

Secret sins are willful, hidden sins may not be willful on the sinner's part, but it happened by a carefully executed plan, by the devil, to rope that person into sin and pin iniquity on them and their bloodline. This will remain, it could remain in a bloodline for generations until someone does spiritual mapping, or prays fervently after the Holy Spirit tells them what went down, and deliverance is had for the sinner that was tricked into sin, or sin was forced on them. Hidden sin is usually done because of *error*. The person may have thought they were okay. They may have thought they were safe. They may have thought they could trust the person or people they were with. They may have thought they were spiritually strong and could function in their dream world and not be overcome by evil, but somehow, they got duped.

Error. They were mistaken and then overtaken. This is often the result of the dry Christian who thinks they don't need to pray, praise, worship, study, or raise an altar. Things are going along okay, and they don't see, usually with their natural senses, anything foreboding coming down the pike, so they are good in their own estimation.

Thinking you don't need to be prayed and praised and paid up is *error*, especially if you are only using your natural senses. What is happening in the spiritual realm is not going to hit the natural realm right away. Things brew in the spiritual realm until they can jump into a person's life and say, Gotcha!

You've got to get out of error and out from under the oppression of the *spirit of error* or a person could make one mistake after another and derail his progress or be blocked completely.

Lying Voices

Staying in *error* could be because of the lying voices that are speaking, either audibly or silently influencing a person or giving them impressions.

"Look at her, she thinks she is so cute. Look at her, she is eyeing your husband." This person may not have even seen your husband, but a *lying spirit* in you wants you unsettled, or angry, to keep you away from that person, that person might be your new best friend, that person might be your destiny helper, that person might be your breakthrough or deliverance. So, what if your husband saw her? What's wrong with your husband? He doesn't want everything he sees or everything that sees him, does he?

Moore than likely that lying *spirit* may want you to miss a divine connection and or have you and your husband fighting tonight.

Error.

A person once asked me about three or four of what turned out to be their favorite ministers, and I believe they each called themselves a prophet. By the Holy Spirit, within minutes of viewing each of the four, I had to turn their broadcasts off. Now it was seen in these "ministry" sessions that they each had a large following. I didn't understand; none of the four were Godly from my discernment. (Thank You, Holy Spirit.)

For each, it was what they *were* saying. The range was from saying something blasphemous to saying nothing of value at all. For one it was the setting and backdrop of his stage. For another, it was what they were wearing. There were many things that gave each away as not being of God. However, mostly it was my spirit man by the Holy Spirit of God simply saying, No!

I told this person, none of these people are of God. I don't know if they were offended or what, but then they recommended a fifth person, who was as bad or worse. His set looked like something straight out of the evil marine kingdom; I couldn't watch it, I just couldn't.

Not only that, after my assessment of each of his favorite "prophets" I found that you could Google and many people have the same impression of these people. Yet, this guy thinks they are great.

This is obviously what he is attracted to: *error*. He is attracted to what they look like; they look polished and nice. Is this man a king? Is he a pharaoh? Then why does he need five prophets?

He is constantly looking for spiritual gifts operating through people, and specifically the prophetic. That is so dangerous to be attracted to. If a person gets a "prophetic" word right even once, he is hooked. Even the weatherman gets it right sometimes, but is the weatherman a prophet?

He is also easily influenced; if there is a crowd applauding, *oohing*, *ahhing*, or looking well off themselves, that's where he aspires to be. The Word of God says we shall know them by their Fruit, not by their "gifts." All the devil has to do then is copy the gifts as Pharaoh's magicians did in the Old Testament.

The devil may try to copy Fruit of the Spirit, but that is hard to do.

Now I realize that this person who knows the Bible and has been studying the Bible for years, wakes up at all hours to take prayer watches and seems to be living upright before the Lord, is in all *error*.

How can this be? And, can I tell him? How can I tell him? And will he believe me? Do I just blurt it out, or try to minister to him by degrees? Only the Holy Spirit knows the answer to that. I prayed to the Lord to know how to proceed, and got the answer, and it was to minister to him first by reasoning and also to find out how deep this error was in this person.

> Come now, and let us reason together, saith the LORD: though your sins be as scarlet, they shall be as white as snow; though they be red like crimson, they shall be as wool. (Isaiah 1:18)

Over some weeks, I tried to reason with him, talking to him, listening to him, but reasoning together wasn't working. He was very rigid in what he believed and also believed he could prove everything he believed by Scriptures in the Bible. His knowledge of the words in the Bible was there, but he interpreted the Bible very literally and not spiritually. This is another indication of not having the Holy Spirit.

Oh, you want an example, don't you? The man of error believe that no one has ever left planet Earth, no one and no spaceships, nothing. Why does he believe that? Because God created the "firmament" and it is *firm* therefore, nothing can penetrate it. That's typical of what he believes and how he interprets Scripture.

Flattery

One needs the Holy Spirit to really understand the Bible, and sometimes that is not even instantaneous; we understand by degrees sometimes and spiritual revelation can take time. Not only that the Word of God is alive, and it can mean something today, but later it could apply to something else another way. The Word of God is not ambiguous; it is dynamic and alive.

(If you don't have the Holy Spirit, you have no idea of what I just wrote.)

Okay, so it was planned by the Holy Spirit that the next time I saw him I was to minister the Holy Spirit to him. Because by his behavior and lack of discernment and in some cases lack of Wisdom, there is no way he has the Holy Spirit.

Folks, it's been nearly a year, and all this person does is avoid me, and that is easy to do because I neither stalk people nor do I beg for anyone's attention. If you don't want to be bothered, I won't bother you. In the same way as mentioned earlier, I could be his destiny helper or a divine connection, that he is avoiding. By the same token, he could be mine. Please know this, just because one is in error or disobedience God won't make the other suffer always; God will provide.

Error is directing his steps, his moves, his associations, and is running and ruining his life.

The absolute worst thing is the ***error*** of a false or counterfeit *holy spirits*. That is another *lying spirit* masquerading itself as the Holy Spirit.

This person sincerely believes he has the Holy Spirit, the genuine article. Besides all of what was just shared, one day I saw him, and he brought me a small gift. He said, "I was out shopping and the Holy Spirit told me to get this for you."

Saints of God, what he brought me is maybe the #1 thing that I hate the most--, like in life. Not only that, but I've also told him that I hate this particular thing. Over the phone I asked him what version of this thing did he get? He told me the version that I agreed to tolerate, but I told him I do not like the other version--, at all. He gives me the gift; it is the #1 thing I hate the most and it is the version that I absolutely cannot stand. I say, "Thank you," because I don't want to alienate him; there is ministry to do here.

Friends, readers, people, God does not hate me and would not tell someone to bring me something that I absolutely hate.

Does this man have the Holy Spirit?

The Holy Spirit is amazing. He is full-force, yet a gentleman. The Holy Spirit is the Spirit of Wisdom, Knowledge, Understanding, Truth. He is your Guide, your Paraclete and so much more. There is no devil or demon, who could even approach the magnitude of the Holy Spirit; they simply do not have the ability or the capacity.

Therefore, we should only listen to the Holy Spirit and not any Voice that is not of God or from God.

For years, if I am unsure of what voice is speaking, I say something like, "Only the Holy Spirit, only the true Holy Spirit can speak to me (right now), all other voices be quiet, or shut up."

Many times, I only have quiet after saying that. After some time, you begin to know the voice of the Holy Spirit and you may not have to say that, but that short prayer declaration is very useful. Amen. Silence evil voices trying to talk to you or lead you astray.

The devil is a liar. He is a copycat and a counterfeiter. Even though the world says that imitation is the sincerest form of flattery, I say, *No, it is not.*

There is a counterfeit holy spirit; who might that demon or that group of demons be trying to flatter? Uh, not the real Holy Spirit. These are fallen angels that cannot be redeemed, so you think they are admiring the Holy Spirit? Hardly. They are attempting to impersonate the real Holy Spirit and usurp His position in your spirit and in your life while hoping the human they are trying to lead into error won't notice. That's not flattery; that is corruption.

The gall, the audacity: Fallen angels try to appear as angels of light. Fallen sons of God try to impersonate God. False Christs try to impersonate Christ, in and out of the dream state, and demonic spirits try to impersonate the Holy Spirit. This should let us know how much we need discernment to navigate all these lies and lying *spirits*.

Sometimes people are jealous of others, and they are not flattering them when they copy them or try to emulate them or steal from them. So, imitation is not the sincerest form of flattery. They are not flattering you when they want what you have, say in an evil exchange where they try to steal your star or your God-given talents, gifts, and virtues. When they want the same car, the same house, the same job, and the same spouse as you, that's not flattery. That's a dangerous person, even if it is your relative.

They may have secret desires like a vulture or a ravenous animal to run you off from your catch, your prize or even to destroy you. Stay prayed up.

Fake Holy Spirit

The Holy Spirit is God, the Third Person of the Godhead. He is the member of the Godhead who does God's work on earth today. Typically, the devil would try to trick and deceive Believers and seekers or would-be Believers by counterfeiting the work and the Person of the Holy Spirit.

Scripture tells us that the devil is a counterfeiter, he is a copycat. Therefore, we can make the following observations:

1. There is a counterfeit *spirit*, maybe more than one.

2. A counterfeit holy spirit is still a spirit, and it tries to occupy the place that the Holy Spirit would live in a man, but it doesn't manifest the qualities, attributes and promises of Jesus after baptism in the Holy Spirit.

(Jeremiah 1:12) That *spirit* is not holy and cannot do what the Holy Spirit does; it is an imposter. If you remember the story of Legion and how 6000 spirits were cast out of him, you may realize the capacity of man to hold *spirits* within himself. The Holy Spirit is huge, powerful, awesome, wise, et cetera and the special place in man for the Holy Spirit is size appropriate for Him.

Lesser and demonic *spirits* are tiny in comparison, although they cause a lot of damage to the soul, spirit, and life of a man.

Most believe the measure of if a person has the Holy Spirit to be whether or not a person speaks in tongues. It is that, but it is more than that.

And while I'm on that subject for those who believe that men can do things in church, in ministry, in God that women can't do--, I challenge you that there is not a different Holy Spirit for women than there is for men. There is no gender in God, first of all, and secondly all there are many gifts and different administrations depending on how the Spirit works in any person --, male or female.

3. There is no Godly power in a counterfeit *holy spirit* (Acts 1:5; 8)

4. There is no fruit of the spirit flowing through a counterfeit *holy spirit*.

5. Spiritual gifts *can be* copied, but they are suspect (I Corinthians 12:7–10; 13). People can fake the Fruit of the Spirit for a while, but soon they will be found out. You know, fake nice people--, you can spot them a mile off.

6. The devil can copy signs and wonders so stop chasing after them. (Mark 16:16–18). So, we need to stop seeking after signs and chasing wonders. The magicians in Pharaoh's court could do magic and snake tricks. The anti-Christ will be able to do signs and wonders and that can deceive many people.

People, magicians who fill auditoriums with their magic acts or entertain at the circus, can do magic; it is a form of witchcraft. That avenue for any antichrist and the final Antichrist has already been laid.

The Holy Spirit has other names that indicate His character, attributes and abilities. He is also called:

- the Anointing,
- the Eternal Spirit,
- the Gift of God,
- the Helper,

- a New Spirit,
- the Oil of Gladness,
- One Spirit,
- the Seal,
- the Spirit of Adoption,
- the Spirit of the Fear of the LORD,
- the Spirit of Holiness,
- the Spirit of Grace,
- the Spirit of Him Who Raised Up Jesus.
- Spirit of Glory.

And there are other names and titles.

The Apostle Paul warned the church at Corinth about counterfeit holy spirits and also false *spirits*. This is Paul who was, when he was Saul, before his conversion was himself, anti-Christ, because he persecuted Christians. After his vision on the Damascus road, he changed completely. After that he was not only teaching and preaching, but he was also a Disciple of Jesus and became an

Apostle. So, I would say his conversion was complete as well as his full deliverance from *error*.

> But now I fear that you will be tricked, just as Eve was tricked by that lying snake. I am afraid that you might stop thinking about Christ in an honest and sincere way. We told you about Jesus, and you received the Holy Spirit and accepted our message. But you let some people tell you about another Jesus. Now you are ready to receive another spirit and accept a different message... Anyway, they are no more than false apostles and dishonest workers. They only pretend to be apostles of Christ. And it is no wonder. Even Satan tries to make himself look like an angel of light. (2 Corinthians 11:3-4, 13-14 CEV)

There are counterfeits to the person of Jesus Christ, there can be a false Jesus. There can be a false gospel message of Christ. There can be false prophets, false pastors, false teachers **as well as a false or counterfeit holy spirit.** They are all counterfeited by the devil for the purpose of leading God's people into *error*, defeat, and or destruction.

Not everyone who uses the words *"Christ," "gospel,"* or *"Holy Spirit"* are of God or from God. It could be the Snake who is speaking, even from a pulpit on a Sunday morning, causing whoever he is using to counterfeit the Truth. Some are just repeating what they heard as kids. Some are really entertainers and are saying what they think will rouse the people. Others are preaching for themselves and trying always to say something clever. And too many are preaching to the offering basket and say only what is convenient for a good offering.

Fakes are not always obvious. Thus, we need to be discerning when we hear the terms, the *Lord Jesus Christ, Gospel*, and *Holy Spirit, Blood of Jesus*. We need to listen closely. Some say, *Christ*, they don't say Lord Jesus Christ. Some don't say the name, *Jesus* at all even while they are ministering. Who do you think this person is introducing you to or leading you to?

Possibly themselves.

Sometimes they say, *the spirit*, but they don't say the Holy Spirit. Sometimes they say blood, but they don't say the Blood of Jesus. I was chastised by an online commentor for not saying, *The Precious Blood of Jesus.*

The precious blood of Jesus is phrased that way once in the entire Bible in the translation that I typically read.

But with the **precious blood** of Christ, as of a lamb without blemish and without spot: (1 Peter 1:19)

The phrase, **the Blood of Jesus** is mentioned 40 times in the Bible, so we don't have to say the word precious every time we mention the Blood of Jesus. But it appears that someone taught that person that??

However, I choose to capitalize the Blood to indicate when I am writing about the Blood of Jesus and to indicate it's importance. Further, I capitalize the Blood of Jesus, and also the Name of Jesus when we use it in spiritual warfare. I do this because both are spiritual weapons, and weapons, especially military weapons are usually capitalized when they are being written about.

Attune your ears and listen, be very discerning.

Test the Spirits

If you hear a word in your heart, in your spirit and your first response is, "Lord, is that You?" That's a better response if you are not absolutely sure than to just believe that *spirit or that voice*. Don't believe the *spirit* just because you heard it and it is a spiritual phenomenon; the devil is also a *spirit*, and his entities are also *spirits*.

Recall, the LORD called Samuel three times before, with the help of Eli, he realized it was the LORD who was calling him and not Eli. The point is, you don't know whose voice is calling you. You don't know who is speaking to you—until you know. Make sure you know and are not just guessing.

> Beloved, do not believe every spirit, but test the spirits to see whether they are from God, because many false prophets

have gone out into the world. (1 John 4:1 NASB)

False prophets have always been out and about. In 1 Kings 13 there was a man of God who came from Judea to Bethel on assignment of the LORD. He did what he was supposed to do and then had previously been told by God, something to the effect of, *Don't go home by the same way you entered into Bethel.*

The young prophet did just as he was told to do. He refused food from the king's table as he had been instructed by God, who had said to him, **"Do not eat or drink anything while you are there."** The young prophet did as he was told and was on his way home when he stopped to rest. But an older prophet caught up with him as he rested The older man **lied** to the young prophet, saying that God had told him to come get the young man and take him home and feed him.

The old prophet was lying.

Folks just because someone has the same job or career as you do, does not make them a truth teller or your buddy. Just as someone could be a divine connection for you, they could conversely be a demonic connection. Try every *spirit*. The devil jumped into Judas while he was seated next to Jesus at supper. The devil tries to get in where he can fit in.

The young man went and ate with the old prophet who then cursed that young prophet telling him that he would not be buried with his ancestors. A prophet can bless or curse, depending on his mission and who sent him. But that curse would not have landed had that young prophet been obedient to God. By his own disobedience that curse was able to alight.

On the way from the old prophet, on the way back to Judea the young prophet was killed by a lion because he disobeyed God.

The Bible account is much more in depth than that. Folks, we need to hear

GOD. Listen to GOD. Turn **ON** Holy Spirit notifications. Do not disobey GOD, do not quench or grieve the Holy Spirit. We discern by the Holy Spirit, but the young prophet's discerner may have been turned off by his flesh which may have been simply hungry. We must **discern** liars, *lying spirits*, false prophecy, and lies--, false pastors, falsehoods. We discern *error*, so we can **LIVE!!!**

The Very Elect

> For there shall arise false Christs, and false prophets, and shall shew great signs and wonders; insomuch that, if it were possible, they shall deceive the very elect. (Matthew 24:24)

I've been deceived more than once, and I've been almost deceived more than once. Speaking of being nearly deceived, had it not been for the Lord sending a true prophetic voice into my life at a critical moment, I would have been tricked by the enemy and possibly also trapped. Or, it could be that I was already captive and, in the hands, or echo chambers of lying voices that lied to me day and night and as often as they could, like a constant drip. Eventually I could have begun to believe their lies, or gotten so tired of them talking that I would have given up or given in.

But God said, **NO**!

This is why we must know the Word of God; we must listen to one-another in ministry. Another saint of God could have the word of salvation, deliverance, and freedom for us, and they could have been sent by the Lord.

How can a person be caught up in *error*? It may not be all at once, it could be a lie here and years later a lie there. It could be a *spirit* that never should have been allowed in got in. That *spirit* could have come with another *spirit* and that one from an unrepented sin. Then one day, five lies coalesce and deceive the person who may be saved, know the Bible, have walked upright with the Lord for years, but this may have been the day, the hour, and the opportunity for the devil to try to harvest a soul that was before that particular day and time, in the Kingdom of God.

In my case the Lion of the Tribe of Judah showed up. What does that even mean? I sensed a *presence* in my home, and it was the presence of a deceased person whom I had loved dearly and respected. That deceased person is not walking the Earth, that was a masquerade. I wasn't grieving the person, or even thinking about them, as they have been deceased for a number of years. So, it's not like I conjured them up, although some over grievers do conjure up *spirits* believing they are their lost loved ones, but they are not. Some people talk to those *spirits* and some listen to those *spirits* talk. I wasn't doing that. This "spirit" had not said anything, but it was as though the "spirit" of that person wanted to tell me something and was hanging around in hopes that I would ask it to speak.

    I did not.

And devils also came out of many, crying out, and saying, Thou art Christ the Son of God. And he rebuking *them* suffered them not to speak: for they knew that he was Christ.
(Luke 4:41)

Folks, this is not a Shakespearean play so there is no reason for a dead person to try to come to me to tell me anything, but yet the devil is always trying to see if and where he can get in.

Now, for the Lion of the Tribe of Judah. I am a seer. In prayer one day or night, I forget the timing of it, a huge lion--, the Lion of the Tribe of Judah came into that room between me and that "spirit" and that Lion just stood there. Day after day, night after night; the Lion did not move but was a barrier between me and that evil *spirit* and the plans of that evil entity.

It was not moving from that position of guarding me from that masquerade. For those who know, this is how I happened to do the Lion of the Tribe of Judah prayers and book; it is because it happened to me. I looked for books on the subject but didn't find much, so I recorded what I had experienced and prayers for others. Jesus Christ, as the Lion of the

Tribe of Judah happened for me, else, I might have been led down a path of *error* and jumped out of the Godly timeline of my destiny.

During that same time period, a prophet was speaking into my life and only said two or three things, over several conversations, that reset two or three *errors* or lies that had been spoken to me that brought instant deliverance as it changed my mind set and reminded me of Truth. Deliverance reminded me of the Truth of God and *error* was dismissed completely.

That entity in that particular masquerade has not entered my environment since. The warfare is not over, though; sometimes I still sense the presence of the Lion of Judah.

The Final Antichrist

The final antichrist will be able to produce lying wonders, and he will do it--, of course he will, But even now, we've got false pastors and prophets in churches, these days, doing all sorts of things under anointing they didn't get from Jehovah GOD. These people have gone around God for anointing. That's super scary because if God didn't or won't anoint them, then they don't need to be anointed; it means that God didn't yet trust them--, or ever would. The reason they have sought that demonic anointing is certainly not for the people of God; it is for their own personal gain. The devil would only agree to it if it would benefit in some way.

Folks, this is why it is so dangerous to look for signs and wonders – the devil can produce those for your entertainment, deception, and destruction.

The final Antichrist, an evil man will come to do the work of Satan with counterfeit power and signs and miracles. He will use every kind of wicked deception to fool those who are on their way to destruction because they previously refused to believe the truth that would save them.

Notice that this individual will produce lying signs and wonders with demonic power. Therefore, if you don't want to be deceived, you must **try** every *spirit*. But know this: everyone who stands in a pulpit or any other seat of authority in the church or government is moving people into *error*, and paving the way for the end time Antichrist.

> But test all things. Hold on to what is good. (1 Thessalonians 5:21 HCSB)

If someone claims to be speaking for God, yet his teaching contradicts God's Word, then that teaching must be rejected. It does not matter if this person can perform signs and wonders.

Some of those "miracles" are staged and fake anyway. How can I say that? Well, I marathon-watched a ministry one long weekend until I couldn't take it anymore. When I started, I was a fan of that ministry and couldn't wait to learn and soak in all that was being taught and presented. By the third hour, the format became predictable. It seemed there was a person from the audience who was called up in each service and they were always wearing a blue blouse or blue shirt. They were always someone in real estate. I'm talking all weekend, I must have watch 10 ministry sessions of this person. I believe in signs and wonders, but I don't believe everything unless the Holy Spirit lets me know it's genuine.

I am also not one to believe TV wrestling moves, either.

For example, when a false person who says they are representing God speaks and they say they are for peace, but really, they are warmongers, then they are liars, and they are not from God.

Test all things.

If that young prophet had tested what the old prophet was telling him instead of relying only on the Word the Lord had given him, that young prophet would have lived.

False Tongues

There is a counterfeit *holy spirit,* so we don't believe everything we see or hear. The Holy Spirit inside of you must bear witness that this thing that you are seeing or hearing is true and is from God. Is it true or not true? We shouldn't necessarily believe someone that when they say that what they are doing or teaching is from the Holy Spirit , even if signs and wonders follow. Unless the teaching is confirmed by the written Word of God, and or the Holy Spirit is bearing witness of its veracity, then it is not true. It should not be received or accepted. In the mouth of two or three witnesses, let every Word be established.

If there is a false holy spirit, then know that there are also false tongues. Everything about this counterfeit is fake, and false.

I saw a story of a false prophet who looks up the members of the church that he is going to minister to on Facebook. Once he gets to the church he then "ministers" to the congregants based on their Facebook posts. He is a fake prophet of lying signs and false wonders. But the people don't know he's doing this, so they are in awe. Remember the person who told me that the Holy Spirit told them to get me a gift that I absolutely hated. The Holy Spirit knows me and would not have done that. So, what false *spirit* or false *holy spirit* does the man of error listen to? What false *holy spirit* is spewing out lies and *error* to anyone of his victims?

Repeating: if there is a false *holy spirit*, and there is, then there can also be false tongues.

Tongues is Scriptural.

To another the working of miracles; to another prophecy; to another discerning of spirits; to another *divers* kinds of tongues; to another the interpretation of tongues: (1 Corinthians 12:10)

There are different kinds and applications of tongues. First, there is your own heavenly language and no one but you and God have any idea what you are talking about. We are supposed to build up our most holy faith by speaking in tongues in our private prayer time.

Now, brethren, if I come unto you speaking with **tongues**, what shall I profit you, except I shall speak to you either by revelation, or by knowledge, or by prophesying, or by doctrine? (1 Corinthians 14:6)

Tongues, your private angelic language is not to be shown off in the congregation. It's just between you and God. If something is not edifying, it doesn't need to be included or spoken.

There are tongues where a message is imparted to a congregation or a group and someone or some people in that group need to hear what God wants to say to them. It is in another whole language that is the language of the people who need to hear that Word. The speaker does not know the language that they are speaking in. It is Holy Ghost inspired; the Holy Spirit knows all languages. The Holy Spirit even understands utterances that are not even words, such as moanings and groanings.

> Likewise the Spirit also helpeth our infirmities: for we know not what we should pray for as we ought: but the Spirit itself maketh intercession for us with groanings which cannot be uttered. (Romans 8:26)

And there is the interpretation of tongues which means that—what was spoken is interpreted by someone else who hears what was spoken. If the person who spoke it also interprets it, they might as well have said it in English or whatever language the people know who are in the group or congregation.

I've been in groups where someone spoke in tongues and someone else stood up to give the interpretation, but the Holy Spirit in me tells me, NOPE, that is not what was spoken. I don't usually have the gift of the interpretation of tongues, and I didn't have the interpretation in these congregations, but I knew in my *knower* that the interpretation that was given was not what was said. The tone of it, the tenor of it was not right. So, I can accept or reject the interpretation because that is **not** what was spoken. You know it in your *knower*. You need to know for yourself so you will know whether to accept or reject the interpretation.

For another reason, it is proved that tongues is a real spiritual gift, else the gift of the Interpretation of Tongues would not be necessary.

If there is no one to interpret the tongues in a congregation, GOD will not release it for the congregation. In that case, if someone got up and spoke in tongues, either the tongues was fake, and should not have been given, or the **interpretation** was wrong or fake. It could have been true tongues for that gathering, but it could have been that the wrong person got up and gave the wrong interpretation while the person with the real gift and the interpretation of what was spoken was disobedient and did not rise and give the correct interpretation.

Lord, You know.

> Have all the gifts of healing? do all speak with **tongues**? do all interpret?
> (1 Corinthians 12:30)

In this particular "church" the person who keeps "interpreting tongues" also both gives and interprets. As well, the message she "interprets" is always flattering to the pastor of that church. Tongues is always about the pastor? I don't think so.

So, ask God.

It is further proof that tongues is real in that it is from God or demonic. Yes, tongues can be demonic. But even if you don't have tongues or the gift of interpretation, the Holy Spirit knows all languages, whether they be of God or not. The Holy Spirit can also give you, by discernment, in your *knower* if what was spoken was generally of God or not of God. One way the Holy Spirit can apprise you of what just happened is that your spirit man could cringe back while hearing ungodly sounds, syllables, or words.

So, this brings us to false tongues. False tongues can emanate from a so-called believer who has a false *holy spirit*. False tongues can have witchcraft ad occultic origins; they are the peeping and muttering sounds of which incantations are made. They are deceptive "tongues" and they are issued by *familiar spirits* and/or the *spirit of peeping and muttering*.

I bring this up because the *error* in this is that the person believes they have the true Holy Spirit. There is error in peeping and muttering., unless they were planning to practice spells, incantations, and witchcraft. The person believes that they have the true Holy Spirit, and they believe they have the gift of speaking in tongues, but this is all false and fake. They believe they are speaking in tongues, but if they are peeping and muttering, that is not tongues. We shall know them by their fruit. And they shall know us by our fruit. This person could be uttering curses.

The term peep means "an unearthly sound; to speak out of the ground."

Thy speech shall be low out of the dust, and thy voice shall be as of one who hath a familiar spirit, out of the ground, and thy speech shall whisper out of the dust.(Isaiah 29:4)

Peeping and muttering are usually very soft, you can barely hear it, but it doesn't sound like full words. It sounds like short and repetitive syllables—like sticky keys on your computer but vocalized. The term mutter refers to "incantations of the Babylonian and Egyptian rituals, magical words."

The other day I saw a video clip of a known prophet--, a very popular man, one of the five favorites of the *man of error* mentioned earlier. He was speaking some peeping and muttering sounds and doing some abra Cadabra type words and movements with his hands. I can't. I just can't. The Holy Spirit in me was grieved and I had to stop watching that immediately and forever. We need the Holy Spirit to keep us from going in paths of *error*.

When you hear sounds like that your spirit man cringes. You draw back; you want to get away from it. It's like nails on a chalkboard, or a high-pitched irritation to your ears, but really it is irritating your spirit man. You want it to stop. You need it to stop.

God gives strong warnings over and again against going to mediums, psychics, fortune tellers, soothsayers, diviners, witch doctors, etcetera.

To the law and the testament, if they speak not according to this word, it is because there is no light in them. (Isaiah 8:20)

Don't Chase Gifts

Herein lies another **error**: People want to know things, they want to know the future, they want to know things that they feel will put them at an advantage in life. For that reason, they may visit a person that they believe is spiritually gifted and able to see into the future or know upcoming events. This is why we don't chase gifts. Many are fooled by signs, wonders, marvels, and spiritual gifts when all those wonders come from a *familiar spirit.*

I went to lunch one day with a group of friends. The waitress would not leave our table, and she talked and talked and talked about the "gifts" in their family. Everything she mentioned was about a *familiar spirit*, but she didn't know this--, she was proud of all this divination. She didn't use the word *divination* because she thought these were gifts. In the same non-ending conversation, she talked about all the troubles and woes in her family, such as fires, floods, all sorts of natural disasters.

We couldn't take it. We each ate about ½ our food and said we had to leave. It was *too much.*

While we were there, I realized that I knew her husband who appeared to be a normal man. He was the chef. This man's mother had started and owned that restaurant for many years before he inherited it. Since then, he had married a whole witch. Did he mean to do that? As Apostle Rodney Chipoyera says, if you marry a witch your entire destiny is shot. *Within a month that restaurant was shut down and those people were gone.* It's been two years now and the place sits empty.

Is it any wonder?

We do not chase gifts in people because people can really be deceived. They can believe that they are speaking for God. If you look in a psychic's *shop*, you may see that they have God stuff in one part of the shop and New Age stuff and occultic paraphernalia in another part of the business. These people really believe they are serving God and that they are helping people and that all of these ways are ways to God. But that is not what Jesus says.

> Jesus saith unto him, I am the way, the truth, and the life: no man cometh unto the Father, but by me. (John 14:6)

This waitress was in no place to hear ministry; the only time she would leave our table is when we spoke about the Lord. Seems *python* had her ears because she couldn't hear us, and she certainly didn't hear her husband who kept trying to pull us away from our table and to get her to *hush*!

Familiar spirits are knowledgeable to a degree; they know about the past. They've been around for ages. They know history, because they were there. They are old; they have existed during the time the witch or divinator is asking about. Anything they seem to know as a forecast of the future comes from 2nd heaven divination; it is not to be trusted. They know all about your deceased relatives and dead loved ones and possibly have firsthand knowledge, since they were there. They are just telling you what happened--, or their *version* of it, for the purposes of the devil. Their goal is to string you along, lie to you, steal from you, derail you and thwart destiny in any way possible.

Don't be the one sitting there grinning and applauding as if this is harmless entertainment. It is not. This is a serious step in the wrong direction if you are trying to reach your God-appointed destiny.

Also, when you visit such a place a *familiar spirit* follows you home and everywhere you go from then on. They were there when your ancestors were living. They aren't channeling; they were there. It is the humans who are channeling from the *familiar spirits* who **KNEW** these people you are asking about. You went there, so if they didn't know where you were before, they have located you now. If the evil covenant that allowed them in your life had expired, by going to this divinator, you just renewed it.

Just the same, unless you get rid of them, *familiar spirits* are also studying you so a generation or two from now when some genius in your family decides to hold a séance or become a medium, they can tell your child, grandchild or great grandchild all about you--, well, what they want them to know about you. THIS IS DEMONIC! These are *lying spirits.* God says that we shouldn't seek them, talk to them, ask them anything, nor listen to them. So, we shouldn't.

Do take note that what they know is from the past, however. To believe what they say as prophecy from GOD is **ERROR**. They are most likely telling you wrong stuff. There could be some truth in it, but mostly there will be lies with a lying agenda.

Now the new problem is that you seek them and not God. Soon, it's a gotcha when they can tell you lie after lie, and you believe it all. A person could fall into all *error* with this kind of information. Handy dandy divinator, your divinator, necromancer, whatever you call them or whatever they call themselves--, they will tell you lots of *stuff*. You end up quenching and grieving the Holy Spirit because you are not listening to Him anymore. You may even stop praying, or you may start praying wrong prayers

> Professing themselves to be wise, they became fools, And changed the glory of the uncorruptible God into an image made like to corruptible man, and to birds, and fourfooted beasts, and

creeping things. Wherefore God also gave them up to uncleanness through the lusts of their own hearts, to dishonour their own bodies between themselves: **Who changed the truth of God into a lie, and worshipped and served the creature more than the Creator, who is blessed for ever. Amen.** (Romans 1:22-25)

Saints of God: sometimes when God speaks, He tells you one thing. Sometimes only one Word and He expects you to search it out. Oh, not a divinator, they will give you an essay, breaking it down as they want, to lead you where they want, and to having you thinking and doing all kinds of things that God never said, never intended. Those things are *error* and that usually leads to destruction.

In the multitude of words there wanteth not sin: but he that refraineth his lips is wise. (Proverbs 10:19)

If that person also does not have other markers of having the Holy Spirit, a person who believes they have the Holy Spirit, even if they speak in other tongues and it sounds like tongues, then perhaps they don't have the true, genuine Holy Spirit.

By *sounding like* speaking in tongues, I don't mean that they should sound like everyone else who speaks in tongues, (although we've heard that too). But when their peeping and muttering and syllables and chopped up sounds sound like it's from another world and doesn't sit right with the spirit that is in you, we may suspect that they don't have the Holy Spirit and therefore are likely to be in error. If they don't have any other markers of having the Holy Spirit, perhaps they don't have the real Holy Spirit.

Knowing this is not to judge them, it is to judge whether you spend time with them, make friends with them, listen to and heed what they say, date them, pray with them or marry them. It is so you can govern yourself accordingly. However, it may be so that you can minister to them, if the Lord says the same.

I've met people who are afraid to receive the Holy Spirit--, they think they may die if they receive Him. They won't. It is not until you receive the Holy Spirit that you will really feel alive.

I've met people who think the Holy Spirit is spooky, so they want no part of Him. He is not spooky. As a matter of fact, He will demystify a lot of things for you that are spooky.

I've met people who think the Holy Spirit and all that speaking in tongues stuff is not necessary; it is only for freaks.

That also is not true; the Holy Spirit is the Person of the Godhead who is ministering in the Earth today. We all need Him.

> But ye, beloved, building up yourselves on your most holy faith, praying in the Holy Ghost (Jude 20)

It is principally between that person and God to know if a person has the Holy Spirit or not, unless God has sent you to minister to them. Pray to the Lord earnestly if you are subjected to, listening to, or sitting under the words, teaching, ministry, or Grace of someone that you suspect doesn't have the Holy Spirit, when they should. You must decide if you can hear from this person, be taught by this person, receive so-called prophecy from this person.

Don't chase gifts; the devil can copy most spiritual gifts and miracles.

A wicked and adulterous generation seeketh after a sign; (Matthew 16:4)

The Antichrist will perform miracles. The Antichrist will be powerful and perform miracles to confirm his false claims of deity and to get followers. The devil will empower him. The devil has power; it is not greater than God's power, but he has power. .

- The Antichrist will call fire from heaven is to make himself appear as divine, powerful and as a prophet. He is trying to emulate

Elijah. To me, this act reinforces my belief that demonic entities don't have Fruit of the Spirit, they don't have empathy or compassion. Neither can they forgive. Elijah shamed and destroyed 450 prophets of Baal on Mount Carmel. To me, it appears that this Antichrist move is payback. It is what a petulant child would do if they got the opportunity. (1 Kings 18:38)

- The Beast receives a fatal wound but is miraculously healed, astounding the world and leading people to worship him. This is fake in order to deceive people into thinking the Antichrist possesses divine power. Not only that. Copycat mode again. Jesus died and was resurrected so the devil wants to try to diminish the power in Jesus' resurrection. Not only that Jesus resurrected several people during His ministry time here on Earth. The devil is competitive and extremely competitive; it is part of the nature of demons. (Revelation 13:3, 12)

These acts are strategic to usurp God's authority and establish his own rule. As a note here, when you see people who have no original ideas of their own but are always copying what others are doing, that is not of God. Creation was God's doing, all God. The devil either wants to copy what God is doing in a I-can-do-it-too showboat-y way, or to tear down the works of God.

Didn't we have childhood playmates like this? Didn't our parents keep us away from those types? We all may be this way with the nature of the devil until we get saved and fully converted.

Attributes of the Holy Spirit

So, we must continue to test the *spirits* because what *spirit* is sent to deceive the whole world is going to come in announcing its demonic assignment? Some other tests are: Compare the characteristics of a *spirit* that is being tested to the attributes of the Holy Spirit. Do they have any characteristics in common? Do you have any of the Fruit of the Spirit? If you don't that means you either do not have the Holy Spirit or you haven't submitted to the Holy Spirit for conversion.

> But the fruit of the Spirit is love, joy, peace, longsuffering, gentleness, goodness, faith,
>
> Meekness, temperance: against such there is no law. (Galatians 5:22-23)

If you don't have the Holy Spirit, you may think that those who have Him are weird. You may think they are weak because the foolish things confound the wise and when we are weak, God in us, the Holy Spirit is strong.

Does the person you are looking at have Wisdom or at least *access* to it?

Do they have discernment? If they don't, in the unsaved world that is called, clueless.

Whether they speak in tongues or not is not as important as the two things I just mentioned. Do they have any Fruit of the Spirit? Do they have at least these two gifts of the Spirit?

But if they do speak in tongues, might as well let the Holy Spirit tell you. Pray about it. Ask the Lord if you have the true and genuine Holy Spirit; be sure you do.

Once you know that you have the Holy Spirit, let Him judge if that is true tongues when you hear tongues, whether you know what they are saying or not, or if that person is speaking a false, peeping and muttering, witchcraft, or demonic type *tongue*. Whether you know what you are saying or not when you pray in tongues, ask the Holy Spirit to make sure it is real and genuine.

A liar will lead you into *error*, loss, destruction or death. Unless you are already in error, *error* would make you believe a liar or someone who is in *error*.

This is why people join and follow cults; they are prone to believe lies. It's as though they love lies or are attracted to and magnetized by them. I personally liken this person to an idolater because they put the liar on a pedestal and follow them faithfully. Many times, they follow evil more faithfully than they follow Christ. It is as though they need lies to urge them on into unrighteousness. They crave it.

If you can't discern that a person is lying, but keep listening to them, the *spirits* that are on that person will be transferred to you. Their lying *spirit*, their false holy spirit, their false prophecy, their false words, their *spirit of deception--*, the whole kit and kaboodle. If you keep sitting under it, it will transfer to you, and you will be like them and very susceptible to do whatever they tell you to do.

You must know the Word of God and have the Holy Spirit. Knowing the Word of God and having the Holy Spirit with discernment helps you separate a lie from truth really quick. Don't sit under it. The longer you listen to a person who is lying to you the more likely you are to be roped into, or fall into *error*.

Fruit of the Spirit

> Then Herod called the Magi secretly and found out from them the exact time the star had appeared. He sent them to Bethlehem and said, "Go and search carefully for the child. As soon as you find him, report to me, so that I too may go and worship him." (Matthew 2:7-8)

Herod was lying, and the Magi knew it.

One way to discern the true Spirit of God from false *spirits* (John 4:1) is to look for the Fruits of the Spirit. You shall know them by their Fruit. (Galatians 5:22-23.) Believe not every spirit. (1 John 4:1-6) The *spirit of the antichrist* and the *spirit of error* (deception) are still at work in the Earth.

If it doesn't make sense to you, if it doesn't make sense to your spirit man, then it is not true. The devil and his agents can also do miracles and healings, so that is no guarantee that they are of God. Is Jesus preached? Jesus, and Him crucified? Jesus resurrected? Is that being preached? Is Jesus being magnified? Is the Blood of Jesus called upon? Does what they are speaking line up with the Word of God? Then they are speaking the Truth. Amen.

A false teacher may really believe himself and be deceived himself. Even the very elect could be deceived. Satan can counterfeit all the gifts and may even use the Name of Jesus (but he will seldom, if ever, use, Lord Jesus Christ). I heard people speak who may not use the name, *Jesus* in their entire message. Now, if they are doing a Ted Talk, that's one thing, but if this is a church and they are supposed to be doing a sermon, what are we talking about here?

The devil cannot copy the *agape* Love of God; it cannot be reproduced or counterfeited. Agape Love cannot be reproduced, neither the Blood of the Lord Jesus Christ & His Resurrection.

False spiritual agents rely on physical sensations and emotional experiences to wow the crowd and fool the people.

Please note how the true Holy Spirit deals with you and do not quench or grieve the Holy Spirit. If the Holy Spirit gives you nausea, for example, when there is something spiritually wrong, then pay attention to it. Don't just get an antacid; pay attention. Pay attention to how the Holy Spirit of God alerts you to lies, deception, falsehoods, false people and *error*. The more you listen to the Holy Spirit the stronger He becomes in your life and the less likely you are to be tricked, deceived or led into *error*.

Until you know, when you see or hear something suspect, evaluate how you feel inside, do you feel creepy, cringy, suspicious? Even if you have a dream and it appears to be a good dream--, how do you feel inside? Do you feel bad, or do you feel good? What your spirit man feels like is a strong indicator of the tone of that dream--, careful, though. That is not always the case; the devil is very deceptive. The Holy Spirit will lead you into all Truth. Now pray and ask the Lord why and what, then be still and listen.

Ask the Holy Spirit, *What was that? What happened? Was that true, was it a masquerade? How do I pray about this?*

Voices

Within yourself, who or what are you listening to? It should be the Voice of God, but there are many more voices that vie for your attention.

Ranked by the most significant and most important to the least are the voices that can influence you.

- The Holy Spirit of God.
- Your own spirit man- which should be led by the Holy Spirit.
- Your soul: Emotions, Will & Intellect.
- The devil and anyone who works with or for him.

Very emotional people let their emotions lead them; they listen to the voice of their emotions which sounds a lot like:

- Ouch! That hurts.
- He hurt my feelings.
- She's not being fair!

Your flesh has a voice and within that at least five other voices since we have five senses. Touch, smell, sight, hearing, taste. Your flesh asks questions such as, "Am I comfortable. What do I want? What would benefit me?"

The soul has a voice, and within it three voices. The voice of the intellect which may sound something like:

- That doesn't make any sense, so I'm not doing it." Or,
- That makes sense so that is the only thing I will do.

The Will has a voice and those who listen to it may be labeled as stubborn or strong-willed. And, the emotions which we have mentioned already.

Devil influences are to convince a man to do something he wouldn't normally do. You must understand God by your **spirit man** while connected to the Holy Spirit. God uses the foolish things to confound the wise. Always seek the Spirit-to-spirit connection.

> It is the spirit of man that will sustain him in trouble (Proverbs 18:14, paraphrased)

There are external voices also. There are the voices of others, voices of friends, and voices of strangers.

People speak out of the *voice* that they are listening to. You can tell by what they say and by their actions just as you can tell what news channels people listen to by their talking points. What's in you is what will come out; out of the abundance of the heart, the mouth will speak, (Proverbs 4:23).

The Spirits that rest on Jesus, are the Seven Spirits around the throne of God. The Holy Spirit.

All these voices are vying for your attention and trying to influence you, direct you, or coerce you into what they want you to do.

Until you realize that you don't know what you're doing, then you don't know what you are doing. The best voice to listen to is the Holy Spirit, the smartest, most Truthful one. We choose all day long, we choose correctly, or we choose *error*. Broad is the way that leads to destruction, narrow is the path of life and few there be that find it.

Whoever you are listening to will influence the advice you may give others and the advice they may give you. Who is your advisor or counselor listening to? Solomon listened to his flesh to marry 700 women and then have 300 concubines.

You train yourself to hear the person you want to hear from. Who you communicate with and spend time with is the voice you get accustomed to. If you are unsaved, your flesh will usually run things, and a person will listen to the voice of whomever is making them happy or giving them what they want. Sex, food, drugs, fame, power, beauty—whatever you're after.

A saved person with a prospered soul, will want to build up their spirit man and not their flesh. That person spends time in the Word of the Lord and begins to know the Lord's Voice. He will begin to know the Lord as Father.

A narcissist will just listen to themselves. People who "listen to their bodies" are listening to their flesh man. But what part of their flesh are they listening to? Depends. Their eyes lust for things and stuff. Their emotions don't want to be hurt and often want revenge. Their ears may like certain things and want to hear those things over and over. Of all the parts of a man the flesh is the most likely to become addicted to things, and most often it is bad things.

The soul also wants to run things, but you have to learn and hear the Voice of the Lord.

My sheep hear my voice, and I know them, and they follow me: 28 And I give unto them eternal life; and they shall never perish, neither shall any man pluck them out of my hand. (John 10:27-28)

The still small voice of the Lord is Mercy. The Voice of God could scare any man because He is God; His Voice thunders. But He, by His lovingkindness comes down to our level. That God would speak to any of us softly, gently is a blessing and a miracle on its own. (see Psalm 29)

A person could lead themselves into *error* by not listening to God and the Holy Spirit. The flesh wants comfort, fun, the flesh wants it now and has no real understanding of **consequences**. The flesh is dumb, people. It could be put in the category of dumb idols. This is especially true of the person who thinks they have the best brain of anyone, and they are always the smartest person in the room.

The person who makes their belly their *god* is not thinking of consequences. When the flesh gets in trouble it does not take responsibility, it just wants relief, and it wants someone to fix it. Now!

Deuteronomy 28 is full of choices and consequences; however, the carnal man doesn't see that. For your consideration: those who cannot see when they are wrong, but they are so good at seeing when others are wrong are supreme beings of carnality; they are carnal people. Those who are not teachable or readily learn life lessons are inherently **carnal people**. Every time you obey your flesh; you build up your flesh and you become more carnal.

If the spirit man is not built up, when a problem arises the flesh man doesn't know what to do. The flesh only knows how to solve things by fighting, running away, eating, drinking or using drugs. Please what other problems has the flesh ever solved? It usually is the cause of problems. The spirit man, through connection with the Holy Spirit solves the problems the flesh creates. Born into sin, born into iniquity, error is all around and waiting to influence the average person.

The more time we spend with God, the more we learn His Voice. The more we obey the Voice of God, the more He will speak to us. The more we pray and praise and worship, and spend time in the Word of God, the more our spirit man will be built up. The less chance we will have to fall into *error* or have error to overtake us.

Real Love

The devil cannot replicate Love. False love is a hallmark of these fake *holy spirit spirits*. It is also a hallmark of fake groups. and it is easily spotted because the leadership may "love" certain ones, but not others. It doesn't mean that no one there has the real Holy Spirit, but often it means they turn off Holy Spirit notifications when they decide to go into the flesh. Fake love is all flesh.

So, these folks may focus on a certain few and not everyone. That attention and fake love is limited to a certain group of folks for whatever reason but not to others. Many times, it is fame, position, and money. Sometimes it is for other nefarious reasons. Sometimes it is all of that.

Don't get roped in because you're the darling this week. That is subject to change quickly and without notice, like the weather.

Cliques are formed and you may be in a clique or want to be in it. This is NOT of God. Leaders of such false groups and false congregations may claim to have the deepest and heaviest revelations of all, more than any other who has ever had a revelation. They may claim that their house of worship is the only place you can get deliverance. They may claim anything--, anything at all. But that does not make it true.

The worst ones don't seem to have a spiritual covering.

This is when you really know that you are going cultish, when you are falling into error is when the group wants to replace your parental authority over your own kids by themselves. They want your kids to obey them more than your kids obey you.

Wives are asked to submit to the group rather than their own husbands. Husbands submit more to the group and tend to the group more than their own wives and families.

The family unit is disrespected.

I know of a church where traditional family holidays are **ignored**. It could be Mother's Day, and everyone is doing whatever they normally do on second Sunday in that place. The female leaders of the place are getting props and gifts and accolades and attention, but the other mothers in the place are basically ignored.

Then after all that, a prayer meeting is called that lasts until 3pm. There is nothing wrong with prayer, but the prayer meeting is a repeat of what already just happened in the regular service except there are no men there. The men? They are in another part of the church also repeating the Sunday service, with no women present. The children?

They are restless, running in and out of the children's room to find out where their mothers or fathers are and asking when will they will be leaving church for home or lunch?

So, it's Mother's Day and folks have been in church for 6 hours, and they make you feel guilty if you don't stay for the "special meetings".

Families are separated. Everyone, including the kids are in "children's church" for the 6th hour. No one has had lunch and Mother's haven't been honored at a traditional Mother's Day dinner or luncheon by their own families. If grandma or grandpa flew in from out of town, they've been ignored, and will continue to be ignored.

The same for Father's Day; they just do whatever they normally do. They don't give honor to the offices that God created, that God created My Bible says we are to honor father and other that it will be well with us and our days will be long on the Earth, except the leaders of that "church." If nothing more, if they show honor to the moms and dads on their respective days, this will teach the children to honor their parents. However, the leaders of the group are acknowledged and gifted on those holidays; people are told how much money to bring for the leader that is to be showcased, and trust me, it's steep. They are told not to bring a gift but bring money. Then everyone else is on lockdown to do the same old thing they do week after week.

You tell me. The leaders of this type of set up have "special revelations" and "deeper truths" than other churches seem to have. They want you to stay there with them. So, the member feels roped into being there, staying there losing their freedom, losing more and more time. Really, they are honoring these leaders more than they are serving God because this is legalism, and God is not requiring any of this. That *group* is requiring it.

My Bible says honor father and mother so your life will be good, and it will be well with you, and you will live a long time.

I've seen such a "meeting" where a question or problem is presented and confusion results until they have to call on the leader to solve the problem and "teach" them the right way because no one in the group can figure out the spiritual problem.

Is that true, or are they playing up to the leader? If it is true, then everyone remains spiritual babies, which is another way to control folks. Wherever you are, have you been growing? If you are not growing spiritually, what are you doing?

The Holy Spirit will not let you remain a spiritual baby or sit in a highchair for feeding when you should be in a full-sized chair, No, you should be standing up and/or teaching others yourself, by now.

Unless you don't have the real Holy Spirit, or you've quenched and grieved the Holy Spirit and now you are in *error* if you are now being taught again, when you should be teaching.

In these control type "churches" sometimes a question is presented to the congregation, and everyone is forced to stand and give an answer, but no one **EVER** gets the right answer. No one. Only that leader knows the right answer. Every time.

Aside from being humiliating, you know this will undermine your confidence over time, right? You know this, right? It is *error*. If you stay in that group for the "deep revelations" you will be spitting out bones trying to get to the fish every day. What happens when you are eating fish, and you miss a bone? What happens if you remain a spiritual baby and you're trying to eat fish and pick out the bones for yourself? First, you have no training in picking out bones. Secondly, you didn't even know there were bones in there; you were not expecting that. Thirdly, how do you even know what a bone is? So, you swallow. Error does not always stand by itself, many times it is mixed with Truth, even "deep revelations." Error is the bone that may try to get hung in your throat while you are trying to partake of the fish.

Of the group that the man of error was fascinated with, at least three of them had some Truth, but where does Truth end and error begin? Only the Word of God and the Holy Spirit can apprise you of that junction or intersection, else, anyone of us could be swallowing bones, getting choked on them, or worse. A telltale sign of a group is in error or prone to error is that group is small or cultish. That may not always be the tell, as I said the men of error--, most of them had a large following, else, how would we know about them except they became very popular?

The error may not be in how they treat the Word. The error could be in how they treat the "church" and the members of the church. Error is a sneaky spirit, we must all be discerning.

Worst case scenario is a counterfeit group will present another Jesus, another *spirit*, another *gospel*. (Gal 1;6, 2 Tim 4:3,4, 2 Cor 2;4)

Sometimes they will deny the Virgin birth, the Blood of Jesus, or the Cross--, but not always. Error can be present and creep in in many other ways. Deny the existence of sin are some other RED FLAGS. Saying God loves you and everyone is going to Heaven no matter how they live here on Earth is like giving a trophy to every T-ball kid no matter how he plays. Well, why would we have to choose life or death, God or not God everyday if it doesn't matter what we choose? Some preach Grace and only Grace. More than likely, that is good for the offering basket. I've met members of churches who are all the happiest people on Earth. They have no problems and expect never to have a problem. The congregation is large and happy and sing and dance to their heart's content every Sunday.

Some preach sin and only sin, which is also *error*. Those congregations are miserable and might as well wear sackcloth and ashes 24/7.

Some may literalize Scriptures such as hate your mother and father (Luke 14:26) As I said, they disrespect the family unit as a means of controlling people. The group that I discussed earlier is big on this passage and they walk it out. How they have the nerve to make people celebrate the leaders with money every year on these parental holidays but then use this Scripture the rest of the year amazes me.

I am in no way trying to discredit your pastor; I don't have anything against your pastor, and I know God needs good under shepherds. Amen. Let this book do more to qualify your pastor rather than disqualify your man or woman of God. Amen.

When it comes to hating relatives, we are not supposed to love anyone more than God. But if someone is a household witch in your family casting spells and doing bewitchments on you, and you've got to deal with them, that's another thing, but I am not talking about that. I'm talking about a regular husband and wife and their two kids. The fact that they are a family is ignored and often they are separated in church is another marker of a cultish-type place.

Didn't the devil try to pit Adam against Eve? Men against the women? That's a sign.

A woman preacher will not go to bed at night without leaving the lights on in her house because she read that the Word says that we shouldn't live in darkness. We need the Holy Spirit to understand Scripture, or we will take it literally.

Another preacher has a sword of the Spirit which she (yes, another woman) walks up and down the aisles of the church during services slicing the air with this sword. She is very literal, and very dangerous.

1. HOLY SPIRIT – true HOLY SPIRIT, we need you.

Use of isolated Scriptures to build weird doctrines by taking things out of context just leads to error and control. You have got to know the Word for yourself, but you must have the TRUE Holy Spirit to understand the Word of GOD. Your pastor will not be angry if you know the Bible; they will be happy because you will be easier to teach.

However, know that some false teachers are deceived, some are spiritualists masquerading as Christians – they are on their assignment.

If the Old Testament is overemphasized and the New Testament is neglected, or vice versa, suspect counterfeit.

There are those who neglect Grace and those who only teach Grace. Balance is needed.

Prayers

2. Father, if I am none of Yours, give me Godly sorrow and a repentant heart for my sins, and make me one of Yours, in the Name of Jesus.

3. Lord, forgive me, the sins of my parents and the sins of my ancestors all the way back to Adam and Eve where I retrieve my glory and my essence, in the Name of Jesus.

4. Lord, cover me in the full armor of God and with the Blood of Jesus for this warfare, in the Name of Jesus.

5. Every devilish, demonic, idol *spirit* in my life, in my soul mimicking the HOLY SPIRIT of GOD, I silence your VOICE in my soul, in my head, in my mind, in the Name of Jesus and I cast you out, out, out, in the Name of JESUS. (X3)

6. Any *spirit* in my soul masquerading as a false *holy spirit*, you are rebuked, you are renounced in the Name of Jesus. Wherever you came from get out of my life and my soul now! in the Name of Jesus.

7. Every guidance and manifestation because of a false *holy spirit* in my life, I reject that guidance and reverse every evil manifestation. I rebuke it the entity that sent it and reverse all negative effects of it, in my life, in the Name of Jesus. (X2)

8. Lord Jesus Christ, who before ascending into Heaven, promised to send the Holy Ghost to finish Your work. Lord grant to me the TRUE Holy Spirit, in the Name of Jesus.

9. Refresh and refill me with new anointing if I already have the true Holy Spirit of God, in the Name of Jesus.

10. Lord, send the Helper.

11. LORD send the Comforter.

12. LORD, send the Paraclete.

13. Lord, send the SPIRIT OF GOD to infill me, to dwell in me to overflowing and to GUIDE and teach me to lead me into all TRUTH in the Name of Jesus. THANK YOU, LORD.

14. Lord, grant me through YOUR SPIRIT: *the Spirit of WISDOM*, that I can say, Wisdom, thou art my sister.

15. Lord, grant me, by Your Spirit, · *the Spirit of UNDERSTANDING*, so that I can say in all my getting, I get Understanding, in the Name of Jesus.

16. Lord, grant me by Your Spirit, *the Spirit of COUNSEL*, so that I am never at a loss for what to do or which way to turn or go, in the Name of Jesus.

17. Lord, by the Holy Spirit of God, grant me the *Spirit of MIGHT* so that I may be very courageous in all things, in the Name of Jesus.

18. ·Lord, impart to me the *Spirit of KNOWLEDGE*, grant it to me, that I never lack Knowledge, in the Name of Jesus.

19. Lord, grant me *the Spirit of the FEAR*, of the LORD. The fear of the Lord is clean, enduring forever. Amen.

20. Seal me, Lord, with the HOLY SPIRIT of PROMISE and that in You I can move and breathe, have my being, and be led into the ways of GOD, to never again into *error*, in the Name of Jesus.

21. Peace *be* unto you: as *my* Father hath sent me, even so send I you. And when he had said this, he breathed on *them*, and saith unto them, Receive ye the Holy Ghost: (John 20:21-22)

22. Holy Spirit of GOD welcome into my life. Welcome. You are welcome here, in the Name of Jesus.

23. Holy Spirit of God for any time I have quenched, ignored, or grieved You, I repent for that. I repent of quenching

or grieving You, in the Name of Jesus. Please forgive me.

24. I repent of turning off Holy Spirit notifications at any time and for any reason in the Name of Jesus.

25. Lord, make my ears attentive to You via the Holy Spirit, make my heart pliable to receive the Word of God, the Word of Truth, in the Name of Jesus.

26. Lord, make me sensitive to reject a lie and *error* in any form, from any source, quickly, in the Name of Jesus.

27. Lord, give me keen discernment to see a lie, to hear a liar, and to reject error, in the Name of Jesus.

28. *Father, today I stand against false teaching false people, false* prophets and false prophecies, in the Name of Jesus.

29. Today I stand against the *spirits of lying, deception & error* trying to take root in my life, in the Name of Jesus.

30. I bind deception, lies and *error* right now, in the Name of Jesus.

31. I curse every attempt of the devil to get me to buy into a lie, in the Name of Jesus

32. I refuse to be tempted to believe lies wrapped in truth and things that sound good or sound right, but do not line up with Your Word.

33. I refuse all sweet talk and false love, in the Name of Jesus.

34. Satan you are a liar, leave me, leave my life now, in the Name of Jesus.

35. Lord, when any person, even those professing to be Christians, exalt new ideas over the Word of God, let me be quick to recognize it, in the Name of Jesus.

36. Lord, let the Holy Spirit bring all Truth to my remembrance that I do not believe a lie, and let me look to Your Word for guidance and confirmation, not to man, in the Name of Jesus.

37. Father, let every veil be removed from my eyes, that I will not be blinded by the opinions of others, by the thoughts and ideas of the world, but I will know the true voice of the Good Shepherd, in the Name of Jesus. Amen.

38. Lord, I ask that You bring conviction upon me for any areas where I have fallen into believing a lie. Show me these areas, and bring them to my mind, that I may know the Truth, repent and be converted, in the Name of Jesus.

39. Lord, I repent of leading anyone into error; show me those instances that I may repent and repair any damage, in the Name of Jesus.

40. Lord, redeem the time and restore the years that believing a lie, lies, or error has wasted and eroded from my life, ministry, and destiny, in the Name of Jesus.

41. Lord, receive my repentance and put me back on the road of Truth, in the Name of Jesus.

42. I reject confusion and I reject *error*, in the Name of Jesus. (X3)

43. I release myself from every *spirit* of confusion and *error*, in the Name of Jesus.

44. Spirit of error, get out of my life. Come up and out, come up and get out, by the power in the Blood of Jesus.

45. I shall know the Truth and the Truth shall make me free, in the Name of Jesus. (X7)

46. Backwardness, constant failures, constant mistakes and *errors*, I break your influence and power over my life, in the Name of Jesus. (X3)

47. Curses that bring errors and mistakes into my life, I break you, I dismantle you by the power in the Blood of Jesus.

48. Whom the son sets free is free; indeed, Lord set me free of *lying spirits*, liars, deceivers, false prophets, false pastors, false people and make me free of *error*, indeed, in the Name of Jesus.

49. *Error*: I find you out, I mark you out, I cancel you and blot you out. I correct every error with the Blood of Jesus, in the Name of Jesus. (X3)

50. Lord, redeem my life from errors, known and unknown, in the Name of Jesus. (X2)

51. Everyone shall bear their own load. By the Blood of Jesus every unconscious covenant with *familiar spirits* in my family is broken and releases me now, in the Name of Jesus. Amen.

52. Father, I cry for Mercy. Son of David, have Mercy on me, in the Name of Jesus.

53. Father, let every altar of witchcraft and *familiar spirit*s and *lying spirits* be

broken, and let the judgment of Heaven come against the evil priest presiding over it, in the Name of Jesus.

54. By the authority of Jesus Christ, I command any evil door that I have opened to witchcraft, *lying spirits*, and *familiar spirits* in any area of my life to be shut and let no man open it ever again, by the Blood of Jesus Christ, Amen.

55. Lord my God, reveal to me every secret of familiar *spirit* attacking me spiritually and physically, in the mighty Name of Jesus Christ.

56. Lord reveal to me every secret of any *lying spirit* that is a poser posing as anything in my life, masquerading as anything in my life or dreams, and remove them by the power in the Blood of Jesus. AMEN.

57. Every blood covenant made with *ancestral spirits, familiar spirits, witchcraft spirits, spirits of divination, python spirits* and *tribal spirits* in my

family and place of birth, be destroyed by the Blood of Jesus.

58. I nullify and cancel the power of any blood sacrifice offered against me, by anyone at any time, in the Name of Jesus. (X2)

59. Lord Jesus, forgive me where I have opened the gates to demonic *spirits* in my life and destiny, in Jesus' Name.

60. I repent of all ignorance, rebellion, and disobedience: Lord, show me *error* that I accepted as Truth, in the Name of Jesus.

61. I repent from all evil agreements and covenants I or any of my ancestors made with *ancestral spirits, familiar spirits*, family strongman, *water spirits*, witchcraft *spirits*, and the occult, in the Name of Jesus.

62. I renounce and cancel every evil agreement and covenant between my life and the evil altars of my family bloodline, in the Name of Jesus Christ.

63. I renounce and reject all the unconscious covenants I have entered with *water spirits, mermaid spirits, dead human spirits and familiar spirits* whether made in the physical, spiritual, or in dreams. I cancel any evil agreement between my life and such *spirits*, in the Name of Jesus.

64. Lord, anything in me that will not spot a *lying spirit*, break that out of me right now, in the Name of Jesus.

65. Any evil covenant that marks me to be lied to, deceived, or fed *error*, break it by the power in the Blood of Jesus, in the Name of Jesus.

66. In the Name of Jesus Christ, I break loose from the power and control of *familiar spirits, mermaid spirits, spiritual wives, spiritual husbands, dead human spirits,* witches, wizards, and satanic agents, in the Name of Jesus.

67. Lord, I retroactively remove my feet from any evil building, house, church,

or meeting where lies and error were being spewed, whether I knew it or not, in the Name of Jesus.

68. Father, by the Spirit of God, I go back in time to when I sat under evil, false, lying, demonic teachers who were masquerading as good and as being from God, but they were not; I withdraw myself from that place, that teaching that person, in Jesus' Name.

69. By the power in the Blood of Jesus I break off any impartation made to me in a false church or setting where the leader or leaders were from the dark kingdom and were deceiving the people as they pretended to be from the Kingdom of Light. Lord, restore me to where I was before I ever entered that place or sat in agreement with anything that was done there and any words that were ever spoken there, in the Name of Jesus.

70. Father, I cover every donation, offering, tithe, seed, or any monetary

instrument placed on the altar of a false "church", lying group, secret society, or demonic group masquerading as a church or a charity that does good for others, with the Blood of Jesus. I cancel that monetary instrument in the Name of Jesus and declare that it was stolen as the pretense of why it was asked for was a lie, in the Name of Jesus.

71. Any evil covenant I have made with money, I break, destroy and rescind my agreement in that covenant, right now, in the Name of Jesus.

72. Lord, I bind every demon sent to enforce an evil covenant and resultant curses against me, in the Name of Jesus.

73. Any evil altar where I have placed an offering or a sacrifice, I remove that sacrifice, I cover my own error of giving to an evil altar with the Blood of Jesus. Lord, I ask for Mercy and forgiveness for participating in such,

whether I did it knowingly or unknowingly, in the Name of Jesus.

74. I break every soul tie with the principal of that place and with the place and any evil people of that place, in the Name of Jesus.

75. Lord, I withdraw my feet from every evil place in the Name of Jesus.

76. Father, I vomit all every error and every evil that was imparted to me, and I replace it with Your Word and with all Truth, in the Name of Jesus.

77. Every evil laying on of hands, in any setting and for any reason, by the Power of Your Christ, reverse the evil impartation made to me, in the Name of Jesus.

78. Any connection whatsoever to liars, lying pastors, false prophets, evil human agents masquerading as angels of light, I sever that connection with them whatsoever. Let them forget my

name and lose my location, forever, in the Name of Jesus.

79. With the Thunder Hammer of God, Lord, destroy the evil altars from any location, any source that are emanating against me, in the Jesus' Name.

80. Lord, I repent of spiritual ignorance, *error*, I repent of disobedience or rebellion and any way I got involved in such, in the Name of Jesus.

81. Lord, make among the very elect that I will not be deceived again, in the Name of Jesus.

82. Lord, give me a heart that will obey You, in the Name of Jesus.

83. Lord, let me run into You that I am protected from all evil, in Jesus' Name.

84. In the Name of Jesus, I curse what God curses, and I bless what the Lord God blesses. I curse evil, I curse lies, and *error*, in the Name of Jesus.

85. Lord, I commend evil agents who deceive God's people to you to be discovered, uncovered, and exposed, and ask the Lord to deal with them according to His Word, His Truth, and His Righteousness, in the Name of Jesus.

86. Thank You Lord for hearing prayers. I seal this Word, these prayers, these decrees and declarations across every dimension, realm age, era, and timeline, past, present and future to infinity in the Name of Jesus.

87. I seal them with the Spirit of God and the Blood of Jesus.

88. Any backlash attempted against any of this Word, this author, the reader, these prayers, these decrees and declarations prayed by anyone any time in the future, backfire with reverb into infinity, and without Mercy against the perpetrator, in the Name of Jesus.

Dear Reader

Thank you for acquiring and reading this book. Let it change your life. Let it help you be sure you are in no way supporting the appearance of the Antichrist.

Not only should you not have to live in *error*, but you also cannot live successfully and reach destiny while operating in error or with it operating in our life. Recognize it, bind it, get it out of your life, in the Name of Jesus.

Shalom,

Dr. Marlene Miles

Prayerbooks by this author

While most books by this author have prayer points either throughout the book or at the end, there are some books that are only prayers. You just open up the book and pray. They are listed below:

Prayers Against Barrenness: *For Success in Business and Life*

Fruit of the Womb: *Prayers Against Barrenness*

Beauty Curses, *Warfare Prayers Against*
https://a.co/d/5Xlc20M

Courts of Marriage: Prayers for Marriage in the Courts of Heaven *(prayerbook)* https://a.co/d/cNAdgAq

Courtroom Warfare @ Midnight
(prayerbook) https://a.co/d/5fc7Qdp

Demonic Cobwebs *(prayerbook)*
https://a.co/d/fp9Oa2H

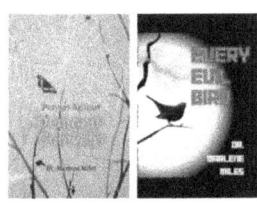

Every Evil Bird https://a.co/d/hF1kh1O

Gates of Thanksgiving

Spirits of Death, Hell & the Grave, Pass Over Me and My House

Throne of Grace: Courtroom Prayer

Warfare Prayer Against Poverty
https://a.co/d/bZ61lYu

Other books by this author

AK: The Adventures of the Agape Kid

Already Married in the Spirit: *Why You May Not Be Married in the Natural*

AMONG SOME THIEVES

Ancestral Powers

Anti-Marriage, *The Spirit of*

Backstabbers https://a.co/d/gi8iBxf

Barrenness, *Prayers Against* https://a.co/d/feUltIs

Battlefield of Marriage, *The*

Beware of the Dog: Prayers Against Dogs in the Dream.

Bless Your Food: *Let the Dining Table be Undefiled*

Blindsided: *Has the Old Man Bewitched You?* https://a.co/d/5O2fLLR

Break Free from Collective Captivity

Broken Spirits & Dry Bones

By Means of a Whorish Father

Casting Down Imaginations

Churchzilla, The Wanna-Be, Supposed-to-be Bride of Christ

Demonic Cobwebs (prayerbook)

Demonic Time Bombs

Demons Hate Questions

Devil Loves Trauma, *The*

Devil Weapons: Unforgiveness, Bitterness,…

The Devourers: Thieves of Darkness 2

Do Not Swear by the Moon

Don't Refuse Me, Lord (4 book series)
https://a.co/d/idP34LG

Dream Defilement

The Emptiers: *Thieves of Darkness, 1*
https://a.co/d/5I4n5mc

Evil Touch

Error (the *spirit* of): Paving the Way for the Antichrist

Failed Assignment

Fantasy Spirit Spouse
https://a.co/d/hW7oYbX

FAT Demons (The): *Breaking Demonic Curses* https://a.co/d/4kP8wV1

The Fold (5-book series)

- The Fold (Book 1)
- Name Your Seed (Book 2)
- The Poor Attitudes of Money (3)
- Do Not Orphan Your Seed (4)
- For the Sake of the Gospel (5)
- My Sowing Journal

Gang Ups: Touch Not God's Anointed

Getting Rid of Evil Spiritual Food

https://a.co/d/i2L3WYQ

got HEALING? Verses for Life

got LOVE? Verses for Life

got HOPE? Verses for Life

got money? https://a.co/d/g2av41N

Here Come the Horns: *Skilled to Destroy*
https://a.co/d/cZiNnkP

Hidden Sins: Hidden Iniquity

https://a.co/d/4Mth0wa

How to Dental Assist

How to Dental Assist2: Be Productive, Not Wasteful

How to STOP Being a Blind Witch or Warlock

I Take It Back

Legacy

Let Me Have A Dollar's Worth
https://a.co/d/h8F8XgE

Level the Playing Field

Living for the NOW of God

Lose My Location
https://a.co/d/crD6mV9

Love Breaks Your Heart

Made Perfect In Love

Man Safari, *The*

Marriage Ed. Rules of Engagement & Marriage

Made Perfect in Love

Money Hunters: Beware of Those

Money on the Altar https://a.co/d/4EqJ2Nr

Mulberry Tree, *The*
https://a.co/d/9nR9rRb

Motherboard (The) - *Soul Prosperity Series*

Name Your Seed

Occupy: *Until I Return*

Plantation Souls

Players Gonna Play

Power Money: Nine Times the Tithe

https://a.co/d/gRt41gy

The Power of Wealth *(forthcoming)*

Powers Above

The Robe, Part 1, The Lessons of Joseph

The Robe, Part II, The Lessons of Joseph

Seasons of Grief

Seasons of Waiting

Seasons of War

Second Marriage, Third--, *Any Marriage*

https://a.co/d/6m6GN4N

Seducing Spirits: Idolatry & Whoredoms

https://a.co/d/4Jq4WEs

Sift You Like Wheat

Six Men Short: What Has Happened to all the Men?

Soul Prosperity soul prosperity series 3

https://a.co/d/5p8YvCN

Souls Captivity soul prosperity series 2

The Spirit of Anti-Marriage

The Spirit of Error: Paving the Way for the Antichrist

The Spirit of Poverty

StarStruck

SUNBLOCK

The Swallowers: *Thieves of Darkness*, 3

Take It Back

This Is NOT That: How to Keep Demons from Coming at You

Time Is of the Essence

Too Many Wives: *Why You Have Lady Problems*

Tormenting Spirits
https://a.co/d/dAogEJf

Toxic Souls

Triangular Power *(series)*

- Powers Above
- SUNBLOCK
- Do Not Swear by the Moon
- STARSTRUCK

Unbreak My Heart: *Don't Let Me Die*

Uncontested Doom

Unguarded Hours, *The*

Unseen Life, *The* (forthcoming)

Upgrade: How to Get Out of Survival Mode

- Toxic Souls (Book 2 of series)
- Legacy (Book 3 of series)

The Wasters: *Thieves of Darkness,* Bk 2
https://a.co/d/bUvI9Jo

What Have You to Declare? What Do You Have With You from Where You've Been?

When I Was A Child, *I Prayed As a Child*

When the Devourer is Rebuked

https://a.co/d/1HVv8oq

The Wilderness Romance *(series)* This series is about conducting a Godly relationship and marriage with someone who is a Wilderness person. It is about how to recognize it and navigate through it. These books are about how not to get caught up in such.

- *The Social Wilderness*
- *The Sexual Wilderness*
- *The Spiritual Wilderness*

Other Series

The Fold (a series on Godly finances)
https://a.co/d/4hz3unj

Soul Prosperity Series https://a.co/d/bz2M42q

Spirit Spouse books
https://a.co/d/9VehDSo
https://a.co/d/97sKOwm

Battlefield of Marriage, The

https://a.co/d/eUDzizO

Players Gonna Play

https://a.co/d/2hzGw3N

Matters of the Heart

Made Perfect in Love
https://a.co/d/7OMQW3O

Love Breaks Your Heart
https://a.co/d/4KvuQLZ

Unbreak My Heart https://a.co/d/84ceZ6M

Broken Spirits & Dry Bones
https://a.co/d/e6iedNP

Thieves of Darkness series

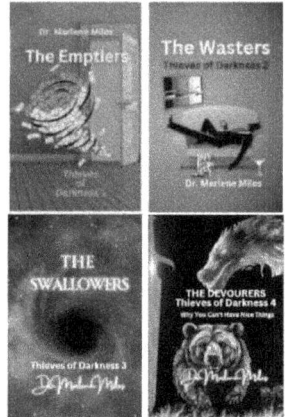

The Emptiers https://a.co/d/heio0dO

The Wasters https://a.co/d/5TG1iNQ

The Swallowers https://a.co/d/1jWhM6G

The Devourers: Why We Can't Have Nice Things https://a.co/d/87Tejbf

Triangular Powers https://a.co/d/aUCjAWC

Upgrade (series) *How to Get Out of Survival Mode* https://a.co/d/aTERhXO

www.ingramcontent.com/pod-product-compliance
Lightning Source LLC
Chambersburg PA
CBHW070201100426
42743CB00013B/3003